BUTTERFLIES IN ROOM 6

WRITTEN AND PHOTOGRAPHED BY
CAROLINE ARNOLD

Butterflies in Room 6

see How They Grow

ini Charlesbridge

Sometimes
the children
see painted lady
butterflies in
the school garden.

THE CHILDREN IN ROOM 6 ARE LEARNING ABOUT BUTTERFLIES.

Their teacher, Mrs. Best, has brought butterfly eggs to school. In about four weeks the tiny eggs will become beautiful painted lady butterflies. How does this happen? The children will watch and find out.

Butterflies help plants grow by carrying pollen from flower to flower. Plants need pollen to make fruit and seeds.

Dozens of butterfly eggs come in a little tube.

The first stage of a butterfly's life is an egg. A painted lady egg looks like a grain of blue salt.

Like many insects, a butterfly has four stages of life. A painted lady's life begins with a small blue egg. The egg becomes a caterpillar, then a pupa, and finally a butterfly.

A larva is the second stage of a butterfly's life. A butterfly larva is also called a caterpillar.

3

The third stage of a butterfly's life is a pupa. A butterfly pupa is covered by a thin shell called a chrysalis. Inside the chrysalis the pupa changes into a butterfly. This process is called metamorphosis.

4

The last stage of a butterfly's life is an adult. A butterfly is an adult insect.

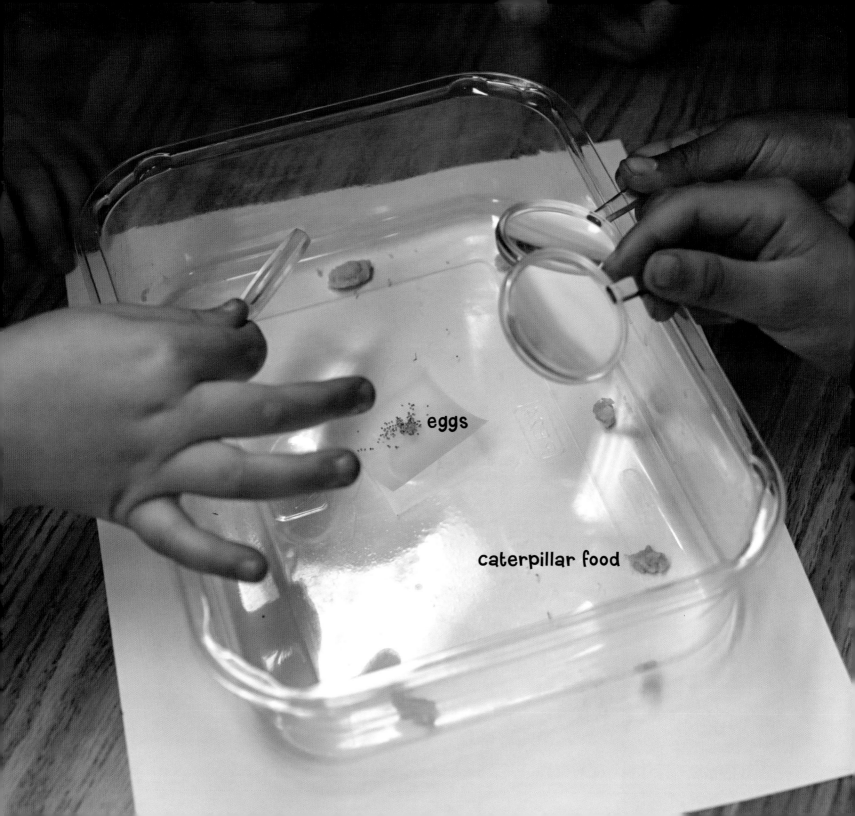

eggs

caterpillar food

Mrs. Best puts the butterfly eggs into a large plastic box. Inside the eggs, caterpillars are growing.

The children add some caterpillar food. After the eggs hatch, the caterpillars will crawl to the food and start eating.

The food is a mix of all the nutrients that painted lady caterpillars need to grow. In the wild they eat leaves.

By the next day the eggs are hatching. The caterpillars crawl out. They look like tiny, dark specks. Each one is smaller than a sesame seed.

The caterpillars eat and eat. Each day they grow a little bigger. The children spread more food on the bottom of the box.

When a caterpillar grows too big for its skin, the skin splits and falls off. A new skin is underneath.

A caterpillar sheds its skin, or molts, several times before it becomes a pupa. Each stage is called an instar.

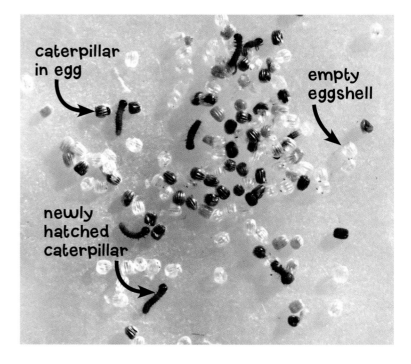

caterpillar in egg

empty eggshell

newly hatched caterpillar

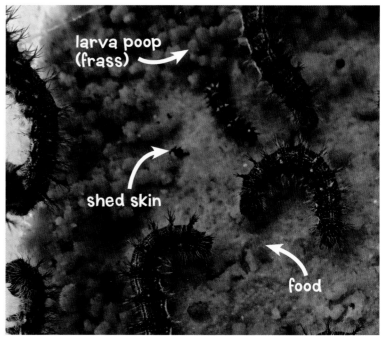

larva poop (frass)

shed skin

food

After a week the caterpillars are about a half inch long. Mrs. Best gently picks up each caterpillar with a paintbrush and puts it into a cup. Small holes in the lid let in air.

The caterpillars keep eating and growing.

Now the caterpillars are two weeks old.
One by one they crawl to the top of the cup
and make a patch of sticky silk on the paper
towel under the lid. The caterpillar attaches
its hind end to the silk and curls up like the
letter J.

The next day the caterpillar sheds its skin
for the last time. It twists and shakes until
the skin slips off. The caterpillar is now a
pupa. It is covered by a soft chrysalis.

Silk comes out of an
opening just below the
caterpillar's mouth.

In a day or so, the chrysalises become hard. Mrs. Best moves them to a flight cage and pins the paper towel to the side.

The chrysalises hang down, just as they would from a leaf or branch. Inside each chrysalis the pupa is transforming into a butterfly.

The flight cage is made of soft netting. When the butterflies come out, they will have room to fly and places to land.

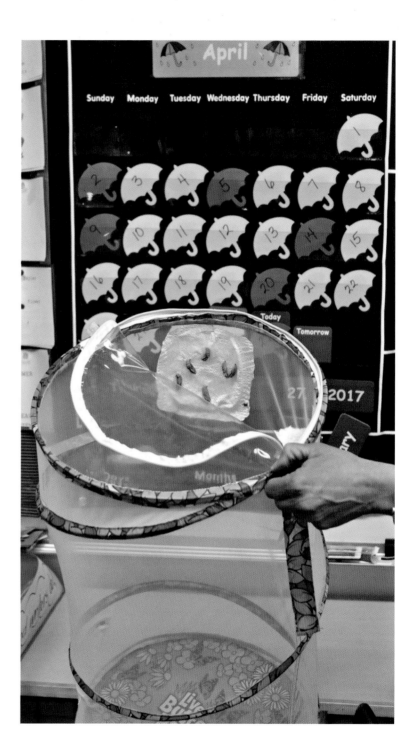

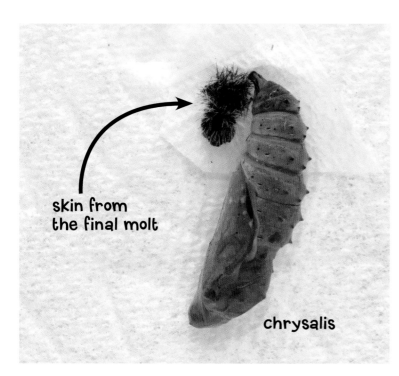

skin from
the final molt

chrysalis

When will the butterflies come out?
The children watch and wait.
Every day they check the chrysalises.
Seven days go by.
No butterflies yet.

When the chrysalis
becomes dark, it is
almost time for the
butterfly to emerge.

On the eighth morning one of the chrysalises is empty. A beautiful butterfly is hanging on the net.

THE BUTTERFLIES ARE COMING OUT!

1 Another butterfly is ready to emerge. Its chrysalis breaks open.

2 The butterfly grabs the paper and pulls itself out. Its wings are wrapped around its body like a closed umbrella.

As soon as the wings are free, they fill with fluid and unfold. They are soft and slightly damp.

The butterfly cannot fly until its wings are straight and stiff. For an hour or so, the butterfly rests as its wings dry.

Butterflies that live outdoors drink flower nectar.

proboscis

The butterflies in Room 6 drink orange juice!

A butterfly drinks with a long tube called a proboscis. It is like a built-in straw that curls up when the butterfly is not using it.

One by one the butterflies come out of their chrysalises. Soon the flight cage is full of butterflies.

The children cut up oranges and slip them into the flight cage. The butterflies sip the sweet juice. The sugar gives them energy.

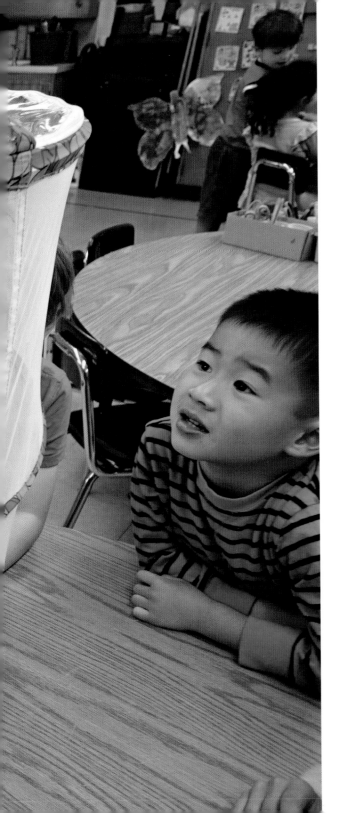

The butterflies flutter their wings and fly inside the flight cage. When they land they hang on to the netting with their feet.

The children wonder which butterflies are boys and which are girls. Males and females look almost the same. Usually females are a little larger and have plumper bodies.

Painted lady butterflies have six legs, like other insects, but they use only four of them. The front pair is small and tucked up behind the butterfly's head.

The children look closely at the butterflies. They see that a butterfly's body is divided into three parts: the head, thorax, and abdomen. On the head are two big eyes and a pair of antennae. The wings and legs are attached to the thorax.

abdomen

hindwing

thorax

forewing

head

A butterfly smells with its antennae. It also uses them for balance when flying.

The eyes are actually clusters of many tiny eyes that help the butterfly see in all directions.

Tiny, colorful scales help make the wings waterproof. The pattern is the same on each side of the body, making the wings symmetrical.

A butterfly tastes with its feet.

A butterfly cannot fly if it is too cold. The outside air must be at least 55 degrees Fahrenheit.

The butterflies are now almost a week old. It is time to let them go.

It is a warm day and not too windy. The children bring the butterflies outside. Mrs. Best reaches into the flight cage and waits for a butterfly to crawl onto her hand.

Mrs. Best slowly brings the butterfly out of the flight cage. The children stand still and hold out their hands. Mrs. Best lets the butterfly crawl from her hand to theirs.

At first the butterfly sits quietly. Then it flutters its wings and flies away.

Each child gets a turn to hold a butterfly. The butterfly hardly weighs anything at all.

When painted lady butterflies are at rest, the pattern on their folded wings helps them hide.

Painted ladies are fast flyers. Their speedy, zigzag flight makes it hard for birds and other predators to catch them.

One by one the butterflies come out of the flight cage.

One by one they fly away.

Some of the butterflies land on flowers. Some fly up into the trees. Some fly over the fence and into the neighborhood.

GOOD-BYE, BUTTERFLIES!

For the next few weeks, the butterflies will feed on flowers, find mates, and lay eggs. When the eggs hatch, the caterpillars will grow into new butterflies.

Perhaps, in a month or so, the children in Room 6 will find more painted ladies spreading their wings and sipping sweet nectar in the school garden.

BUTTERFLY QUESTIONS

Do you have to start with eggs to raise butterflies?

No. Most people start with caterpillars. You can order caterpillars and food from a supplier. If you find a painted lady caterpillar, you may be able to raise it by feeding it leaves. Thistle and hollyhock leaves are preferred.

How does a pupa become a butterfly?

Inside the chrysalis most of the pupa's body dissolves and becomes liquid. It then regrows into a butterfly, using the liquid as nourishment.

What are the red stains on the side of the flight cage?

Shortly after a butterfly emerges from its chrysalis, it ejects meconium, a red liquid left over from metamorphosis.

How long do painted lady butterflies live?

They usually live for only a few weeks. If you raise butterflies, it is best to release them after a few days.

How do you hold a butterfly?

Let the butterfly crawl onto you. It will fly away when it is ready. Never touch a butterfly's wings. The delicate scales will rub off.

What is the difference between a butterfly and a moth?

Butterflies are typically more colorful than moths and have antennae with rounded ends. Most moths have thin or feathery antennae. Butterflies are usually active during the day, while moths are mostly active at night. A butterfly pupa is covered by a chrysalis. The covering of a moth pupa is called a cocoon.

Painted lady butterflies live on every continent except Antarctica and Australia.

BUTTERFLY VOCABULARY

abdomen: the rear segment of an insect's body.

adult: the final stage of an insect's life.

antenna (plural, antennae): a feeler on an insect's head used for smell and balance.

caterpillar: the larval stage of a butterfly or moth.

chrysalis (plural, chrysalises or chrysalides): a butterfly pupa; or the hard outer covering of the pupa.

egg: the first stage of an insect's life.

frass: body waste produced by a caterpillar or other insect.

head: the front part of an insect's body.

instar: a stage of caterpillar growth in between molts.

larva (plural, larvae): the young form of a butterfly, moth, or other insect.

meconium: a red liquid produced during metamorphosis and ejected by the butterfly after it emerges from its chrysalis.

metamorphosis: a change in shape and habits, such as when a caterpillar becomes a butterfly.

molt: to shed, as when a caterpillar sheds its skin.

nectar: a sugary liquid produced by flowers.

pollen: a fine powder, usually yellow, produced by flowers and used to make seeds.

proboscis: the flexible tube used by a butterfly, moth, or other insect for sucking nectar.

pupa (plural, pupae): the resting stage of an insect as it transforms from larva to adult.

silk: a liquid made by caterpillars that turns to a solid thread in the air.

thorax: the middle segment of an insect's body, to which its legs and wings are attached.

BUTTERFLIES ONLINE

The Life Cycle of
Painted Lady Butterflies
https://www.youtube.com/watch?v=63B1lnqPa8k
Time-lapse video of painted lady butterflies raised in a second-grade classroom.

Painted Lady Butterfly Care Sheet
http://www.carolina.com/teacher-resources/
Document/painted-lady-butterfly-care-handling-instructions/tr10531.tr
Useful information about raising painted lady butterflies, including answers to common questions.

10 Fascinating Facts About Butterflies
https://www.thoughtco.com/facts-about-painted-lady-butterflies-1968172
https://www.thoughtco.com/fascinating-facts-about-butterflies-1968171
Facts about painted ladies, the most widely distributed butterfly in the world, and about butterflies in general.

Butterflies and Moths of
North America: Painted Lady
https://www.butterfliesandmoths.org/species/
Vanessa-cardui
Map, information, and photos of painted lady butterflies in North America.

FURTHER READING ABOUT BUTTERFLIES

Butterflies by Seymour Simon (HarperCollins, 2011)
Basic facts about butterflies.

Face to Face with Butterflies by Darlyne Murawski (National Geographic, 2010)
Facts and firsthand experience from a butterfly scientist and photographer.

Fly, Butterfly by Bonnie Bader (Grosset and Dunlap, 2014)
The life cycle and migration of a monarch butterfly.

From Caterpillar to Butterfly by Deborah Heiligman (HarperCollins, revised edition 2015)
Illustrated story about a classroom raising a painted lady caterpillar in a jar.

Handle with Care: An Unusual Butterfly Journey by Loree Griffin Burns (Millbrook, 2014)
A visit to a butterfly farm in Costa Rica.

The URLs listed here were accurate at publication, but websites often change. If a URL doesn't work, you can use the internet to find more information.

ACKNOWLEDGMENTS

I thank Jennifer Best and her kindergarten students at Haynes Charter for Enriched Studies, Los Angeles, California, for sharing the wonder of metamorphosis with me. Their excitement was contagious as they watched the caterpillars transform into beautiful butterflies before releasing them outdoors. I am grateful to the children's parents and the school principal, Barbara Meade, for their enthusiastic support, and I thank my husband, Art Arnold, for his help with the photography. Most of all, I appreciate Jennifer's cheerful cooperation on this project. I couldn't have done this book without her. Jennifer ordered the eggs, food, and flight cage from Carolina Biological Supply Company, one of several companies that offer materials for raising butterflies.

To Jennifer Best, her students,
and their families

First paperback edition 2024
Copyright © 2019 by Caroline Arnold

Published by Charlesbridge
9 Galen Street
Watertown, MA 02472
(617) 926-0329
www.charlesbridge.com

Library of Congress Cataloging-in-Publication Data
Names: Arnold, Caroline, author, photographer.
Title: Butterflies in Room 6: see how they grow/written and photographed
    by Caroline Arnold.
Other titles: Butterflies in room six
Description: Watertown, MA: Charlesbridge, [2019] | Includes
    bibliographical references.
Identifiers: LCCN 2017055927 | ISBN 9781580898942 (reinforced for library use) |
    ISBN 9781623542672 (paperback) | ISBN 9781632897671 (ebook)
Subjects: LCSH: Painted lady (Insect)—Life cycles—Juvenile literature. |
    Butterflies as pets—Juvenile literature.
Classification: LCC QL561.N9 A76 2018 | DDC 638/.5789—dc23
    LC record available at https://lccn.loc.gov/2017055927

Printed in China
(hc) 10 9 8 7 6 5 4
(pb) 10 9 8 7 6 5 4 3 2 1

Display type set in Swung Note by PintassilgoPrints, Family Dog Fat
    by Pizzadude.dk, and Poplar by Barbara Lind
Text type set in Jesterday by Jelloween Foundry
Color separations by Colourscan Print Co Pte Ltd, Singapore
Printed by 1010 Printing International Limited in Huizhou, Guangdong, China
Production supervision by Brian G. Walker
Designed by Susan Mallory Sherman and Sarah Richards Taylor